The Divine Springtime

A collection of spiritual and poetic thoughts

Compiled by Juliet Grainger
Paintings by Chris Rowan Grainger

Courtesy of Llewellyn Alexander (Fine Paintings) London
www.Llewellynalexander.com

 Intellect

In memory of my father Eric Harvey, who loved the beauty of words.

Contents

Nature

The Divine Springtime is come.

Bestir thyself and magnify before the entire creation the name of God and celebrate His praise, in such wise that all created things may be regenerated and made new.

This is the Day whereon the unseen world crieth out "Great is thy blessedness O earth, for thou hast been made the foot-stool of thy God.

Baha'u'llah

Rise up, my love, my fair one, and come away, for lo, the winter is past, the rain is over and gone; the flowers appear on the earth, the time of the singing of birds is come, and the voice of the turtle is heard in our land.

Song of Solomon

Blessed is the spot, and the house and the place, and the city, and the heart, and the mountain, and the refuge, and the cave, and the valley, and the land, and the sea, and the island, and the meadow where mention of God hath been made, and His praise glorified.

Bahai Prayer

I wandered lonely as a cloud
That floats on high o'er vales and hills
When all at once I saw a crowd,
A host, of golden daffodils:
Beside the lake, beneath the trees,
Fluttering and dancing in the breeze.

I wandered lonely as a cloud

William Wordsworth

Fair daffodils, we weep to see
You haste away so soon;
As yet the early rising sun
Has not attained his noon.
Stay stay,
Until the hasting day
Has run.

Robert Herrick

When we were in the woods beyond Gowbarrow Park we saw a few daffodils close to the waterside. But as we went along there were more and yet more and at last under the boughs of the trees, we saw that there was a long belt of them along the shore, about the breadth of a county turnpike road. I never saw daffodils so beautiful. They grew among the mossy stones about them. Some rested their heads upon these stones as a pillow for weariness and the rest tossed and reeled and danced and seemed as if they verily laughed with the wind that blew upon them over the lake.

Dorothy Wordsworth

Slowly, silently, now the moon,
Walks the night in her silver shoon.

Walter de la Mare

A thing of beauty is a joy for ever:
Its loveliness increases; it will never
Pass into nothingness; but still will keep
A bower quiet for us, and a sleep
Full of sweet dreams, and health and quiet breathing.

John Keats

Know ye not that ye are the temple of God, and that the spirit of God dwelleth in you.

Corinthians 3

O Son of Man
The temple of being is my throne;
Cleanse it of all things, that I may be
established and there I may abide.

Baha'u'llah

Every man of discernment, while walking upon the earth, feeleth indeed abashed inasmuch as he is fully aware that the thing which is the source of his prosperity, his wealth, his might, his exaltation, his advancement and power as ordained by God, is the very earth which is trodden beneath the feet of all men.

The whole universe reflecteth His glory.
This is what is meant by divine unity.

Baha'u'llah

He leadeth me beside the still waters. He restoreth my soul

Psalm 23

Neath the shade of Thy protecting wings let me nestle and cast
upon me the glance of Thine all protecting eye.

Abdu'l-Baha

Nature is painting for us day after day pictures of infinite beauty

John Ruskin

The wonders of His bounty can never cease, and the stream of His merciful grace can never be arrested.

Baha'u'llah

The sound of the wind in the trees speaks to me as an inner voice. The breath of life fills me.

Juliet

I expand and live in the warm day like corn and melons.

Ralph Waldo Emerson

Consider the flowers of a garden: though differing in kind, colour, form and shape, yet inasmuch as they are refreshed by the waters of one spring, revived by the breath of one wind, invigorated by the rays of one sun, this diversity increaseth their charm and addeth unto their beauty.

Abdu'l-Baha

There is one mind common to all individual men. Every man is an inlet to the same and to all of the same. Who hath access to this universal mind is a party to all that is or can be done, for this is the only sovereign agent.

Ralph Waldo Emerson

Each sees in the other the Beauty of God reflected in the soul, and finding this point of similarity, they are attracted to one another in love. This love will make all men the waves of one sea, this love will make them all the stars of one heaven and the fruits of one tree.

Abdu'l-Baha

And there are diversities of operations, but it is the same God which worketh in all.

Corinthians 12

Breathing in, I calm my body
Breathing out I smile.
Dwelling in the present moment.
I know this is the only moment.

Thich Nhat Hanh

The beauty of the deer with that long lingering look, the mew of the
buzzard, the hum of the bee and the turquoise dart of the dragonfly,
fill my soul with the perfection of our creation and the wonder of
being alive.

Juliet

God is speaking through his creation.

In the wildlife garden of Glastonbury Abbey

If it be Thy pleasure make me to grow as a tender herb in the meadows of Thy grace, that the gentle winds of Thy will may stir me up and bend me into conformity with Thy pleasure, in such wise that my movement and my stillness may be wholly directed by Thee.

Baha'u'llah

To bear fruit,
the branch must stay united with the vine.

John 15.4

Every created thing in the whole universe is but a door leading into His Knowledge, a sign of His sovereignty, a revelation of His names, a symbol of His majesty, a token of His power, a means of admittance into His straight path.

Baha'u'llah

Nobody sees a flower – really – it is so small
It takes time - we haven't time – and to see takes time,
like to have a friend takes time. If you take a flower in
your hand and really look at it it's your world, for the moment.

Georgia O' Keefe

The portals of Thy grace have throughout eternity been open, and the means of access unto Thy presence made available unto all created things.

Baha'u'llah

The kiss of the sun for pardon,
The song of the birds for mirth,
One is nearer God's heart in a garden
Than anywhere else on earth.

Dorothy Frances Gurney

Every blade of grass has an Angel that bends over it
and whispers, "Grow, grow."

The Talmud

All the atoms of the earth bear witness, O my Lord to the greatness of
Thy power and of Thy Sovereignty and all the signs of the universe attest
the glory of Thy majesty and of Thy might.

Baha'u'llah

A sprinkling from the unfathomed deep of His sovereign and all-pervasive Will hath, out of utter nothingness, called into being a creation which is infinite in its range and deathless in its duration.

Baha'u'llah

I am Alpha and Omega –
The First and the Last.

Revelation 22.13

What life can compare to this?
Sitting quietly by the window, I watch the leaves fall, and the flowers bloom, as the seasons come and go.

Hsueh-Tou

Verily I say the creation of God embraceth worlds besides this world, and creatures apart from these creatures.

Baha'u'llah

....it is only the finite that has wrought and suffered,
The infinite lies stretched in smiling repose.

Ralph Waldo Emerson

The process of His creation hath no beginning and no end.

Baha'u'llah

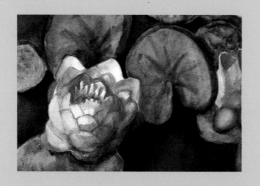

Calm

There is a silence into which the world cannot intrude.
There is an ancient peace you carry in your heart and have not lost.

A Course in Miracles

There are so few empty hours in the day or empty rooms in
my life in which to stand alone and find myself. Too many
activities, and people and things, and interesting people.
For it is not merely the trivial which clutters our lives but the
important as well.
We can have a surfeit of treasures...

Ann Morrow Lindbergh

If material anxiety envelops you in a dark cloud, spiritual radiance lightens your path.

Abdu'l-Baha

Lighten our darkness, we beseech thee O Lord; and by thy great mercy defend us from all perils and dangers of this night.

Christian Book of Common Prayer

When a thought of war comes, oppose it by a stronger thought of peace.
A thought of hatred must be destroyed by a more powerful thought of
love.

Abdu'l-Baha

May peace and peace and peace be everywhere.

The Upanishads.

If you desire with all your heart friendship with every
race on earth, your thought, spiritual and positive, will spread;
it will become the desire of others, growing stronger and stronger.

Abdu'l-Baha

The purest and most thoughtful minds are those that
love colour the most.

John Ruskin

You do not need to leave your room...
Remain sitting at your table and listen,
Do not even listen, simply wait.
Do not even wait, be quite still and solitary.
The world will freely offer itself to be unmasked.
It has no choice.
It will roll in ecstasy at your feet.

Franz Kafka

To see a World in a Grain of Sand,
And a Heaven in a Wild Flower,
Hold infinity in the palm of your hand,
And eternity in an hour.

William Blake

As a man thinks in his heart so he is.

Proverbs 23

Thou my babe! Shalt wander like a breeze. By lakes and sandy shores, beneath the crags of ancient mountains and beneath the clouds... So shall thou see and hear the lovely shapes and sounds intelligible of that eternal language which thy God utters.

Samuel Taylor Coleridge

He leadeth me beside the still waters. He restoreth my soul.

Psalm 23. 2-3

Refresh and gladden my spirit. Purify my heart.
Illumine my powers.
I lay all my affairs in Thy hand,
Thou art my guide and my refuge.
I will no longer be sorrowful and grieved;
I will be a happy and joyful being.

Abdu'l-Baha

Listen in deep silence;
Be very still and open your mind...
Sink deep into peace
That waits for you beyond the frantic, riotous thoughts
And sights
And sounds of this insane world.

A Course in Miracles

Come away from the din.
Come away to the quiet fields over which the great sky stretches and where, between us and the stars,
There lies but silence,
And there in the stillness, let us listen to the voice that is speaking within us.

Jerome K. Jerome

The peace of God, which passeth all understanding, keep your hearts and minds in the knowledge and love of God.

Book of Common Prayer

Arranging a bowl of flowers in the morning can give a sense of quiet in a crowded day – Like writing a poem or saying a prayer.

Ann Morrow Lindburgh

Not for a moment hath His grace been withheld nor have the showers of His loving- kindness ceased to rain upon mankind.

Baha'u'llah

Let my doing nothing when I have nothing to do become untroubled to its depth of peace like the evening on the seashore when the water is silent.

Rabindrath Tagore

Better than a thousand useless words is a single word that gives peace,

The Dhammapada

Trust in him at all times....Pour out your heart to him, hold nothing back.

Psalm 62.8

Naps are the adult version of a child's fort. A love of privacy and a place for make-believe. Rest adds strength to our souls.

Sark

Be content with what you have; rejoice in the way things are. When you realize there is nothing lacking, the whole world belongs to you.

Lao-tzu

Rely upon God, trust in Him, praise Him and call Him continually to mind. He verily turneth trouble into ease and sorrow into solace and toil into utter peace.

Abdu'l -Baha

Over all the mountaintops is peace.
In all the treetops you perceive
scarcely a breath. The little birds in the forest are silent.
Wait then; soon you, too, will have peace.

Johan Wolfgang von Goethe.

If I keep a green bough in my heart, the singing bird will come.

Anon

We don't need to go to China to enjoy the blue sky. We don't have to travel into the future to enjoy our breathing. We can be in touch with these things right now.

Thich – Nhat Hanh

I dream'd in a dream I saw a city invincible to the attacks of the whole of the rest of the earth, I dream'd that was the new city of Friends.

Walt Whitman

And join with thee
calm
peace
and quiet.

John Milton

He who smiles rather than rages is always the stronger.

Japanese Wisdom

Speak ye to Him with gentle speech.

Abdu'l-Baha

Turn your face away from the contemplation of your own finite selves and fix your eye upon the Everlasting Radiance; then will your souls receive in full measure the Divine Power of the Spirit and Blessings of the Infinite Bounty.

Abdu'l-Baha

The process of His creation hath no beginning and no end.

Psalm 46.10

Rest thou assured that in this era of the spirit, the Kingdom of Peace will raise up its tabernacle on the summits of the world, and the commandments of the Prince of Peace will so dominate the arteries and nerves of every people as to draw into its sheltering shade all the nations on earth. From springs of love and truth and unity will the true Shepherd give His sheep to drink.

Abdu'l-Baha

Love

Put love in the world
and heaven with all its beatitudes and glories
becomes a reality.
Love is everything; it is the key of life and its influences
are those that move the world.

R.W. Trine

But the love will have been enough; all those impulses of love return
to the love that made them. Even memory is not necessary for love.
There is a land of the living and a land of the dead, and the bridge is
love, the only survival, the only meaning.

Thornton Wilder

I loved thy creation,
Hence I created thee.
Wherefore do thou love Me,
That I may name thy name and fill
thy soul with the spirit of life.

Baha'u'llah

I have found the paradox that if I love until it hurts, then
there is not hurt, but only more love.

Mother Teresa

Love is heaven's kindly light, the Holy Spirit's eternal breath that vivifieth the human soul.

Abdu'l-Baha

This above all – to thine own self be true,
And it must follow, as the night the day,
Thou canst not then be false to any man.

William Shakespeare

Plant naught but the rose of love,
in the garden of Thy heart.

Baha'u'llah

A rose by any other name would smell as sweet.

William Shakespeare

Love gives life to the lifeless.
Love lights a flame in the heart that is cold.
Love brings hope to the hopeless and
gladdens the hearts of the sorrowful.

Abd'ul-Baha

Love is not love
Which alters when it alteration finds
Or bends with the remover to remove.
O no, it is an ever-fix'ed mark,
That looks on tempests and is never shaken.

William Shakespeare

Make of me a hollow reed
from which the pith of self hath been blown;
that I may be a clear channel for Thy Love
to flow through to others.

Anon

When across the flooded weirs the wild-fowl fly,
When the dead leaves fall from each remembered tree,
When over the withered grass the plovers cry,
I will come back to you and you to me.

John Cowper Powys

Love Me
That I may love thee,
If thou lovest Me not,
My love can in no wise reach thee.

Baha'u'llah

Is prayer your steering wheel, or your spare tyre?

Corrie Ten Boom

It was only a glad "Good Morning,"
As she passed along the way;
But it spread the morning's glory
Over the livelong day.

A.H. Japp

There is a comfort in the strength of love;
'Twill make a thing endurable,
Which else would overset the brain,
Or break the heart.

W. B. Carpenter

Love is the breath of the Holy Spirit
in the heart of man.

Love is light
no matter in what abode it dwelleth.

What a power is love.
It is the most wonderful the greatest
of all living powers.

Abdu'l-Baha

He will never reach the heart
Who has not learned to listen.

W.B. Carpenter

There are no 'white' or 'coloured'
signs on the foxholes or
graveyards of battle.

John F. Kennedy

Do all the good you can,
By all the means you can,
In all the ways you can,
In all the places you can,
At all the times you can,
To all the people you can,
As long as ever you can.

John Wesley

Be calm, be strong,
be grateful and become
a lamp full of light,
that the darkness of sorrows be annihilated
and that the sun of everlasting joy arise
from the dawning place of the heart and soul
shining brightly.

Abdu'l-Baha

Armed with the power of Thy name
Nothing can ever hurt me,
And with Thy love in my heart
All the world's afflictions
Can in no wise alarm me.

Baha'u'llah

Lives of great men all remind us we can make our lives sublime,
And departing, leave behind us
Footprints on the sands of time.

Henry W. Longfellow

Standing as I do, in the view of God and eternity, I realise that patriotism is not enough. I must have no hatred or bitterness towards anyone.

Edith Cavill

Spoken to the Chaplain who attended her before her execution by firing squad. 12th October 1915.

Then Peter came to him and asked, 'Lord, how often am I to forgive my brother if he goes on wronging me? As many as seven times?' Jesus replied, 'I do not say seven times but seventy times seven.'

Matthew 18

Where there is great love,
there are always great miracles.

(Notice above the door of the leprasorium, Calcutta)

The pure heart is a heart that is free, free to give,
to love until it hurts.
The pure heart is a heart that serves, that loves God
with undivided love.

Love more every day. Love till it hurts.

Mother Teresa

My prayer for you is that you may grow in holiness through love for one another – for where there is love there is peace, there is joy. So keep the joy of loving one another in your hearts, and share this joy with all you meet.

Mother Teresa

Inasmuch as ye have done it unto one of the least of these my brethren, you have done it unto me,

Matthew 25.40

Release love into every situation
and see what happens.
To release love
you have to fill your consciousness with
loving, positive, constructive thoughts,
you have to transform every seeming negative situation into a positive one.
But do it quickly.

Eileen Caddy

Be as a lamp unto them that walk in darkness,
a joy to the sorrowful,
a sea for the thirsty,
a haven for the distressed,
an upholder and defender of the victim of oppression.

Baha'u'llah

Healing

All shall be well and all shall be well, and all manner of things
shall be well.

Dame Julian of Norwich

O Lord my God and my Haven in my distress!
My shield and my shelter in my woes!
My Asylum and Refuge in time of need,
And in my loneliness my companion.

Abdu'l-Baha

No matter what happens always be thankful,
For this is God's will for you.......

Thessalonians 5

Many candles can be kindled from one candle
Without diminishing it.

The Talmud

The candle of thine heart is lighted by the hand of My power,
Quench it not with the contrary winds of self and passion.
The healer of all thine ills is remembrance of Me.

Baha'u'llah

Keep your face to the sunshine and you cannot see the shadow.

Helen Keller

If I can stop one heart from breaking,
I shall not live in vain.
If I can ease one life that is aching
Or cool one pain;
Or help one fainting robin
Unto his nest again,
I shall not live in vain.

Emily Dickenson

With a nod
He layeth balm on every wound.
With a glimpse
He freeth the heart from the shackles of grief.

Grant that this broken-winged bird attain a refuge and
shelter in Thy divine nest.

Abdu'l-Baha

Thy Name is my healing, O my God, and remembrance of Thee
is my remedy. Nearness to Thee is my hope, and love for Thee is my
companion. Thy mercy to me is my healing and my succour in both
this world and the world to come. Thou, verily, art the All- Bountiful,
The All-Knowing, the All-Wise.

Baha'u'llah

Healing means to make whole, to accept all parts of ourselves, not just the parts we like, but all of us.

The body like everything else in life is a mirror of your inner thoughts and beliefs. Every cell responds to every single thought you think and every word you speak.

Start listening to what you say. If you hear yourself using negative or limiting words change them.

Louise L. Haye

7. *Selections from Rizvan Tablet Malaysian Baha'I Prayer Book p85*
9. *Song of Solomon . The Bible Old Testament'*
   Baha'i prayer book . Malaysian p3 1996.
11. *William Wordsworth 1807 Oxford book of quotes*
    Robert Herrick 1591- 1674 .The Medici Soc. Ltd
13. *Dorothy Wordsworth 1771-1855. The Grasmere Journals 15 Apr. 1802*
15. *Walter de la Mare 1873-1956.Silver. Oxford book of quotations.*
    John Keats 1795-1821 bk 1.11 Oxford book of quotations
    John Ruskin. 1819-1900. Reflections on the way we see.
17. *The Bible. New Testament 1 Corinthians v.3-6*
    The Hidden words. No. 58. Intellect books.
19. *Tokens. Baha'I Pulishing Trust Wilmette, Illinois. pp53,19.*
21. *The Bible. Old Testament. Psalm 23*
    Compilations of Baha'i Prayers p30
    R.W.Emerson Chap.6 idealism Nature.
    John Ruskin Fall Branch New River Quote 1819 1900
23. *Abdu'l Baha. Gleanings p61*
    Juliet Grainger
25. *Selections from the Writings of Abdul Baha. P291*
    Ralph Waldo Emerson 1803-1882. iv Spiritual Lairs.
27. *Love. Jewels from the words of Abdu'l Baha. 1994 Baha'i Publishing Trust.*
    The Bible. New Testament. 1 Corinthians v. 12-6
29. *Thich Nhat Hanh. Suffering is Not Enough..*
    Juliet Grainger
31. *Prayers and Mediatations by Baha'u'llah p240*
    The Bible, New Testament. John 15.4
33. *Tokens.Baha'I Publishing Trust, Wilmette, Ilinois p9*

References

Georgia O'Keefe. Ref. flickr website.
35. Tokens. Baha'i Publishing Trust, Wilmette, Illinois p23
Dorothy Frances Gurney 1858-1932. God's Garden. Oxford Book of Quotations.
37. The Talmud. Judaism. Growing Towards the Light. Royal   Falcon Books. 2006
Tokens. Baha'i Publishing Trust, Wilmette, Illinois 1973 p29
39. Ibid p11
The Bible. Revelation 22.13
41. Hsueh-Tou 982-1052 Chinese Master. One Hundred Koans.
Tokens. Baha'i Publishing Trust, Wilmette, Illinois 1973 p13..
43 Thirty Day Mental Diet. Science of | Mind Publications 1984
Tokens. The Baha'i Publishing Trust, Wilmette, Illinois 1973 p11
47. A Course in Miracles. Silence
Gift From the Sea.
49 Abdu'l Baha. Paris Talks p111
Christian Book of Common Prayer
51 Abdul Baha. Paris Talks p29
The Upanishads. C 900-600
Abdu'l Baha. Paris Talks p39..
53. John Ruskin 1819-1900. The Stones of Venice vol.1 chap 2.
Franz Kafka.1823-1924. The quotation page. The biography of Franz Kafka.
55. Auguries of Innocence. Oxford Book of Quotations.
The Bible. Old Testament. Proverbs 23
57. Samuel Taylor Coleridge 1772-1834. Sonnet to a friend.
The Bible. Old Testament. Psalm 23.
59. Malaysian Baha'I Prayer Book. 1996 Baha'I Publishing Trust. Prayer 61.
A Course in Miracles. Zen moments.
61. Jerome K. Jerome 1859-1927 Oxford Book of Quotations.

References

Christian Book of Common Prayer.
63. Gift From the Sea. 1966-2001
    Gleanings from the Writings of Baha'u'llah p18
65. Rabindrath Tagore. Stray Birds 1916. New York Macmillan Co.
    The Dhammapada. Dhammapada – atthakatha. Buddhism   guide - attkakatha.
67. The Bible. Old Testament. Psalm 62.
    Sark. Change Your Life Without Getting Out of Bed.
69. Lao-tzu 6th C BC
    Selections From the Writings of Abdul Baha. P178
71. Johan Wolfgang von Goethe 1749-1832.
    Anon.
73. Thich-Nhat Hanh.Suffering is Not Enough.
    Walt Whitman 1819-1892. I dream'd in a dream. Oxford Book of Quotations.
75. John Milton 1608-1674. Penseroso 1.45 Oxford Book of Quotations
    Anon
    Abdu'l Baha. The Secret of Divine Civilisation p53
77. Abdu'l Baha. PARIS Talks p166.
    The Bible. Old Testament. Psalm 46
79. Selections from the Writings of Abd'ul-Baha p246
83. The Bond of Sympathy. London Bailey Bros. Ltd. 1922
    The Bridge of San Luis Rey. Longman Green and Co. 1928
85. Hidden Words. No. 4. Intellect Books
    The Best Gift is Love. Fount Harper Collins 1982
87. Love. Jewels from Abdu'l Baha.1996 Baha'i Publishing Trust,
    William Shakespeare. Hamlet. RSC Shakespeare 2007
89. Hidden Words. No.3 Part 2 (From the Persian). Intellect Books.
    William Shakespeare. Romeo and Juliet.The RSC Shakespeare 2007

References

91. *Love. Jewels from Abdu'l Baha p.7. 1994 Baha'i Publishing Trust.*
     William Shakespeare. Sonnet no. 116. The RSC Shakespeare 2007
93. *Anon*
     John Cowper Powys. November. Samphire. Thomas Seltzer, New York.1922.
95. *Hidden Words. No.5. Intellect Books.*
     Corrie Ten Boom. corrie ten boom @ world prayr.
97. *A.H.. Japp. The Bond of Sympathy. London Bailey Bros. Ltd. 1922.*
     W.B. Carpenter. Ibid
99. *Love. Jewels from Abdu'l Baha 1994. Baha'i Publishing Trust.*
101. *W.B. Carpenter. The Bond of Sympathy. Ibid*
     John F. Kennedy. From a speech while visiting the Berlin Wall.

References

First Published in the UK in 2010 by Intellect Books, The Mill,
Parnall Road, Fishponds, Bristol, BS16 3JG, UK

First published in the USA in 2010 by Intellect Books, The
University of Chicago Press, 1427 E. 60th Street, Chicago, IL
60637, USA

A catalogue record for this book is available from the British
Library.

Publisher: Masoud Yazdani
Book Design: Belle Ward
Paintings by: Chris Rowan Grainger
  Courtesy of Llewellyn Alexander (Fine Paintings) London
  www.Llewellynalexander.com
Compiled by: Juliet Grainger

ISBN 978-1-84150-350-9

Printed and bound by Orchard Press Cheltenham Ltd, Tewkesbury, UK.